OUR WORLD

AMAZING
BEACHES

by Maria Spalliero

NATIONAL
GEOGRAPHIC
LEARNING

CENGAGE
Learning

Almost everyone loves beach vacations. But there are many different kinds of beaches and beach vacations. For example, some people like big resort hotels. Others would rather go to isolated beaches where there aren't many people. People also go to the beach for different reasons. Some go to relax. Others go to explore and be active.

If you could choose any type of beach vacation, where would you go? Grab your passport, your sunglasses, and some sunscreen, and let's visit some of the world's most interesting and amazing beaches.

Beaches with soft, white sand are very popular all over the world. The beach with the whitest sand in the world may be Hyams Beach in Australia. At least that's what the *Guinness Book of World Records* says. The sand on this beach is so white because it is made of tiny particles of quartz crystal.

However, not all sand is white. The color of sand depends on the minerals in it. Sand is made when waves move over and erode, or wear away, minerals in rocks. Over time, billions of tiny particles of rock and other materials, such as seashells, create a beach.

Iron oxide (rust) makes the sand red on the beaches of Prince Edward Island in Canada.

Tiny bits of red seashells mix with white sand to make the beaches of Bermuda pink.

Some sand is even black! In places with volcanoes, sand may be formed by lava that cools in the water.

If you went to a beach like Punalu'u in Hawaii, you would have to wear sandals. The black sand absorbs the sun's heat, making it extremely hot in the daytime. The sand could actually burn your feet!

But people don't just go to beaches for the sand. They also go for the water!

The water in the Dead Sea, which is between Israel and Jordan, is special. It's ten times saltier than the ocean. It's so thick with salt that fish can't live there, and people float easily on the surface.

Many tourists believe the minerals in the salt and the mud from the shores of the Dead Sea are healthy. These people come to the Dead Sea to swim and rub the mud on their skin.

If you were more interested in big city fun than in mineral baths, then you'd probably like the beaches of Rio de Janeiro, Brazil.

Rio is the most visited city in the Southern Hemisphere. Two of its extremely popular beaches are Copacabana and Ipanema. These two beaches are the sites of huge celebrations, especially on New Year's Eve and during Carnival, a festival held every February. Even on regular days, these beaches are busy with swimmers, sunbathers, and people selling food, drinks, and souvenirs.

Just relaxing on the beach is not enough for some vacationers.

Water sports like surfing are popular with many beach visitors. In fact, when you visit the beaches of Tahiti, an island in Polynesia, you may want to bring a surfboard. Otherwise, you might be one of the only people not surfing!

Sometimes the surfers on these beaches ride waves that are enormous!

While surfers ride on top of the water, other beachgoers would rather see what's underneath.

Snorkeling and scuba diving are fun activities that many people do on beaches near coral reefs. The reefs are not only beautiful, but they are also home to many types of tropical fish.

Bonaire, an island in the Netherlands Antilles, is considered one of the best sites for diving and snorkeling because of its clear waters and protected reefs.

If you wanted a beach vacation that focused more on wildlife, you might want to visit the Galápagos Islands. Over 965 kilometers (600 miles) from South America, these 19 islands were extremely isolated for thousands of years. The islands' wildlife includes species of animals that are not found anywhere else on Earth!

Species include the marine iguana, the Galápagos giant tortoise, and many unusual birds, including the only penguins that live in a tropical area.

Because the islands are so isolated, the animals never learned to fear people, so they often come right up to visiting tourists.

The Galápagos Islands are a protected area. Only a limited number of tourists can visit at one time, and visitors must stay with a guide and be careful not to interfere with the wildlife.

Now that you've taken a tour of some of the world's most amazing beaches, which type of beach would you like to visit?

Facts About Coral Reefs

Not far below the surface of the ocean lie colorful, large, rock-like structures called coral reefs. Many kinds of fish live in coral reefs. These reefs are found in tropical ocean waters around the world. Most reefs are between 5,000 and 10,000 years old. Some began as long as 50 million years ago!

What Are Coral Reefs Made Of?

Coral reefs are made of thousands of tiny, tube-shaped animals called corals, or polyps. These animals are related to jellyfish but are much smaller. Most polyps are less than 2.5 centimeters (1 inch) in size. Corals get food from colorful algae, or tiny plants, that live on the coral. The algae give corals their beautiful colors, such as blue, red, yellow, orange, and green.

How Do Coral Reefs Form?

A reef begins to form when a polyp attaches to something hard lying on the floor of the ocean. Before long, the polyp splits into thousands of other polyps. These connect to one another and form one large group of corals called a colony. These colonies grow and join together to form reefs over thousands of years.

Why Are Coral Reefs Important?

Coral reefs cover less than 0.2% of the ocean floor. Yet coral reefs are home to at least 25% of all sea life on our planet! The reefs protect the sea creatures and provide them with food. But many reefs are in danger. If the reefs are not protected, much of the original coral reef areas could be lost forever.

Word Play · Beach Vacations

Use the clues to fill in the crossword puzzle with the correct words.

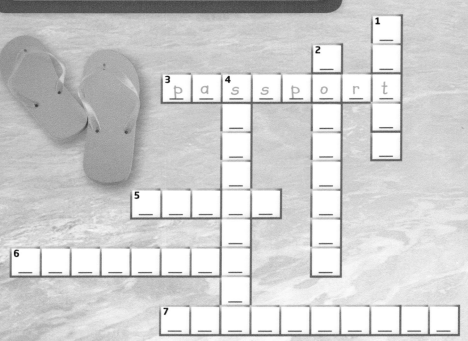

Across

3. An official document that proves a person's country of citizenship.

5. A place with sand and water.

6. Animals that live in nature.

7. Something people wear to protect their eyes from the sun.

Down

1. A place where people stay when they are on vacation.

2. A thing that is kept as a reminder of a place.

4. A lotion people wear to protect their skin.

Look at the picture. Imagine where the girls are and why they are there. Use your imagination to write a short paragraph about them. Try to use as many of the words below as possible.

beach   hotel   passport   resort   souvenir
sunglasses   sunscreen   tour   wildlife

Glossary

coral a structure built from the hard skeletons of a tiny sea animal

crystal a type of rock that is clear or light-colored and has many flat sides

erode to wear away little by little; to break down slowly

float to stay on the surface, or top, of water

interfere with bother

isolated very far away or removed from other places or people; remote

minerals non-living things that are formed in the earth, such as rocks or salt

particles very small grains or pieces of something, like dust or sand

quartz a clear or white crystal

reefs walls or lines of rocks or corals under the water

scuba diving diving deep under the surface of the water using a mask, fins, and an oxygen tank for breathing

snorkeling swimming face down using a tube for breathing and a mask to look under the water

surface top or upper part

tropical being in a part of the world that is very warm